Pet Care

Guinea Pigs

Bobbie Kalman & Kelley MacAulay

Photographs by Marc Crabtree

Crabtree Publishing Company

www.crabtreebooks.com

A Bobbie Kalman Book

Dedicated by Kelley MacAulay
For Victoria Lee, a wonderful friend

Editor-in-Chief
Bobbie Kalman

Writing team
Bobbie Kalman
Kelley MacAulay

Substantive editor
Kathryn Smithyman

Project editor
Rebecca Sjonger

Editor
Molly Aloian

Art director
Robert MacGregor

Design
Margaret Amy Reiach

Production coordinator
Heather Fitzpatrick

Photo research
Crystal Foxton
Kristina Lundblad

Consultant
Dr. Michael A. Dutton, DVM, DABVP
Exotic and Bird Clinic of New Hampshire
www.exoticandbirdclinic.com

Special thanks to
Devan Cruickshanks, Brody Cruickshanks, Heather and Tim
Cruickshanks, Steve Cruickshanks, Kyle Foxton, Doug Foxton,
Aimee Lefebvre, Alissa Lefebvre, Jacquie Lefebvre, Jeremy Payne,
Dave Payne, Kathy Middleton, Natasha Barrett, Mike Cipryk
and PETLAND

Photographs
Marc Crabtree: back cover, title page, pages 3, 5, 6, 7, 10,
    11, 13, 14, 15, 16-17, 19, 21 (left and bottom right), 22, 23,
    24, 25 (wood pieces), 26, 30, 31
Robert MacGregor: page 25 (except wood pieces)
Other images by Digital Vision, Comstock, and PhotoDisc

Illustrations
All illustrations by Bonna Rouse

Digital prepress
Embassy Graphics

Printer
Worzalla Publishing Company

Crabtree Publishing Company

www.crabtreebooks.com   1-800-387-7650

PMB 16A
350 Fifth Avenue
Suite 3308
New York, NY
10118

612 Welland Avenue
St. Catharines
Ontario
Canada
L2M 5V6

73 Lime Walk
Headington
Oxford
OX3 7AD
United Kingdom

Cataloging-in-Publication Data
Kalman, Bobbie.
  Guinea pigs / Bobbie Kalman & Kelley MacAulay;
photographs by Marc
Crabtree.
     p. cm. -- (Pet care series)
  Includes index.
  ISBN 0-7787-1755-0 (RLB) -- ISBN 0-7787-1787-9 (pbk.)
  1. Guinea pigs as pets--Juvenile literature. [1. Guinea pigs.
2. Pets.]. I. MacAulay, Kelley. II. Crabtree, Marc, ill. III. Title.
IV. Series.
  SF549.G9K25 2004
  636.935'92--dc22
                                                    2003027239
                                                    LC

Contents

What are guinea pigs?

Guinea pigs are **mammals**. Mammals have fur or hair on their bodies. They also have backbones. Mother mammals make milk inside their bodies to feed their babies. Guinea pigs are part of a group of mammals called **rodents**. Most rodents have small bodies and sharp front teeth that never stop growing.

A guinea pig's body

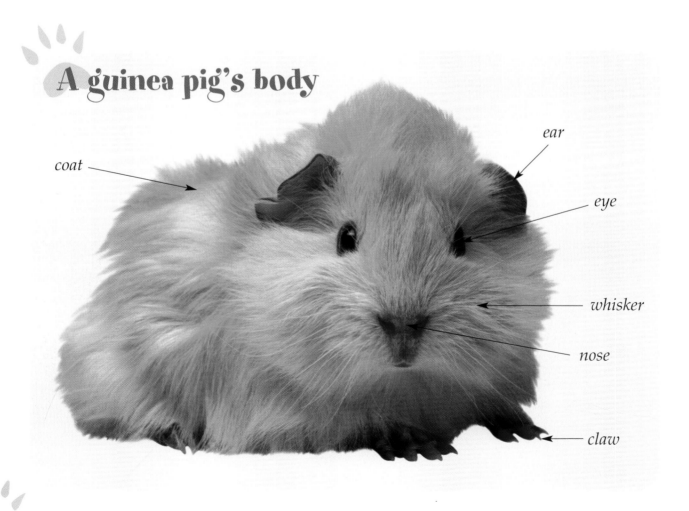

coat

ear

eye

whisker

nose

claw

Roaming relatives

Guinea pigs are not actually pigs! They are related to **wild cavies**. These animals live in the mountains and grasslands of South America. Pet guinea pigs are known as cavies, too! Wild cavies do not live with people. They live outdoors in large groups called **herds**. Wild cavies build their homes in **burrows**, or tunnels. Pet cavies are similar to wild cavies, but they live at home with you.

Pet guinea pigs do not have burrows, but they still like to have warm, dark places for sleeping. Your guinea pigs will need a sleeping box filled with hay.

The right pet for you?

Guinea pigs make great pets because they are cute, cuddly, and friendly. They love to spend time with people! Caring for your guinea pigs can be a lot of work, however. They will depend on you for food and affection every day. You will need an adult to help you **groom**, or clean, your guinea pigs and tidy their cage.

A lasting friendship

Guinea pigs usually live from five to seven years. You will need to care for your guinea pigs as they grow older.

Are you ready?

The questions below will help you and your family decide if you are ready to own guinea pigs.

- A guinea pig does not like being alone. It should always have another guinea pig to live with. Is your family willing to pay for the care of two guinea pigs?

- Do you have time to play with your guinea pigs and cuddle them every day?

- Guinea pigs need to be kept in a large cage. Do you have room for one in your home?

- Will you take care of your pets for many years?

- Guinea pigs like to look pretty! Do you have time to groom your guinea pigs?

- Is anyone in your family **allergic** to guinea pigs?

Guinea pigs galore!

There are many **breeds**, or kinds, of guinea pigs. **Purebred** guinea pigs have parents and grandparents that are the same breed. **Crossbred** guinea pigs have parents or grandparents that are different breeds. Purebreds are the most expensive guinea pigs to buy. The biggest difference between breeds is the length of the guinea pigs' coats. Some of the most popular breeds are shown on these pages.

*Abyssinians have coats that grow in **crests**, or swirls, all over their bodies! They look very fluffy.*

Peruvians have long, silky coats. They must be brushed every day.

Shelties have long coats, but the fur on their faces remains short. Shorter fur helps these guinea pigs see where they are going!

Satins have silky coats that feel smooth when you touch them.

Baby guinea pigs

Baby guinea pigs are called **puppies**.
Up to four puppies are born together
in a **litter**, or group, of puppies. Newborn
puppies look like very small adult guinea
pigs. They are covered in fur when they
are born. The puppies can even see and
hear! They are full of energy
and love to run and jump.

*Guinea pigs feel safe
when they are together.
The puppies snuggle
close to their mother
when they go to sleep.*

Time with mom

Puppies need to be with their mother for five
weeks so she can feed them and keep them
warm. The puppies drink their mother's milk
until they are three weeks old. Never take
a puppy away from its mother too early!

Puppy love

Guinea pigs can have babies of their own when they are only four weeks old! Male and female guinea pigs should be separated after four weeks to make sure they do not have more puppies. There are already many guinea pigs that need good homes!

Baby guinea pigs are very cute, but remember that they will soon grow up. Adult guinea pigs are just as sweet and fun!

Picking your guinea pigs

To find pet guinea pigs, check your local **animal shelter**, or ask friends and family if they know of any guinea pigs that are being given away. You can also buy your guinea pigs from a pet store or a **breeder**. Make sure you get your pets from people who take very good care of their animals.

What to look for

Your guinea pigs will be loving friends for years. The list below will help you choose happy, healthy guinea pigs.

 bright, clear eyes

 clean ears

 thick, shiny coats

 dry, warm noses

 clean backsides

Fun with friends

Remember that guinea pigs get lonely, so you will need at least two. It is best to find two female guinea pigs that are already friends. Keep in mind that two male guinea pigs living in the same cage may fight. If the guinea pigs are older, choose two that already live together.

When choosing baby guinea pigs, pick two that are from the same litter.

Preparing for your pets

Before you bring your guinea pigs home, get everything ready for your new pets. Some of the things that you will need to care for your guinea pigs properly are shown on these pages.

Guinea pigs like to be warm. They need a sleeping box filled with hay.

*Your guinea pigs need a large cage or a **hutch** in which to live.*

*Buy a bag of **bedding**, such as aspen shavings, for the bottom of the cage.*

*Set up a **litter box** in one corner of the cage with fresh litter in it.*

Use a **ceramic** food bowl so your guinea pigs cannot chew it or knock it over.

Guinea pigs sleep in hay, but they also like to eat it. Set up a hay box with fresh hay for munching.

Guinea pigs need fruit-tree branches for **gnawing**. Gnawing stops their teeth from growing too long.

You need a brush to keep your guinea pigs looking great.

A water bottle will hold clean water for your guinea pigs.

Guinea pigs get bored easily. Make sure they have toys to play with.

Home sweet home

You can buy your guinea pigs' cage at a pet store. Make sure it is set up before you bring your pets home. Guinea pigs are active animals, so they need a large cage. Choose one with wire mesh to make sure your pets get a lot of fresh air. Never keep your guinea pigs in a fish tank! When choosing a cage, look for one with a metal floor. A wire floor would hurt your guinea pigs' feet.

sleeping box filled with hay

Cover the bottom of the cage with clean paper and then add a thick layer of aspen shavings. Never use cedar or pine shavings. These woods could make your pets very sick.

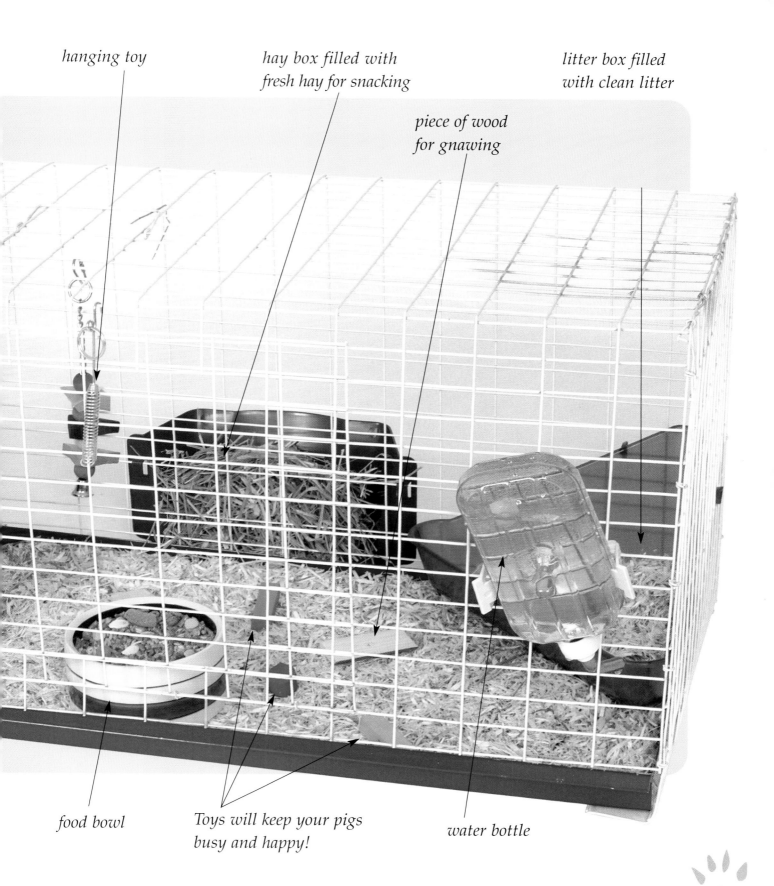

hanging toy

hay box filled with
fresh hay for snacking

litter box filled
with clean litter

piece of wood
for gnawing

food bowl

Toys will keep your pigs
busy and happy!

water bottle

Welcome home!

Your new pets will be scared when you first bring them home. Put your guinea pigs in their cage and leave them alone for a few hours. Not playing with them may be hard, but you will have much more fun with your pets after they feel comfortable.

If you have other pets, they may be curious about your new animals. Ask an adult before you introduce your guinea pigs to another pet. Never leave another animal alone with your guinea pigs.

Not so noisy!

Guinea pigs are easily frightened. Never yell at your guinea pigs or at others in the room where your pets live. Do not run and jump in the room, either. If you are calm, your pets will soon feel safe and loved when you are there.

Your guinea pigs will love to cuddle up in your warm lap!

Gentle cuddles

You must be very gentle while holding your pets. To put a guinea pig in your lap, place one hand under its chest and the other around its bottom. Never squeeze or drop your pet! If it squirms, carefully put it back on the floor.

What's for dinner?

Guinea pigs need a variety of foods to be healthy. You can buy food made just for guinea pigs at a pet store. Ask your **veterinarian** or "vet" which brand to buy. Packaged guinea pig food is a mixture of grains, seeds, and pellets. Adult guinea pigs need to be fed twice a day.

Today's special

Your guinea pigs will need fresh fruits and vegetables every day. Make sure the foods have been washed. An adult can help you cut the food into small pieces. Here are a few guinea pig favorites that will keep your pets strong and healthy.

apple

carrots

broccoli

cucumber

pears

Fresh water

Your guinea pigs need plenty of water to keep them healthy. Make sure their bottle is always full of fresh water. Clean the bottle every day and check it for leaks.

Not for dinner

Even though your guinea pigs like some of the foods you eat, be careful not to feed them something that will make them sick!

- Never give chocolate to your pets.

- Never feed meat to your guinea pigs.

- If you have other pets, never feed their food to your guinea pigs.

Keeping clean

Guinea pigs lick their coats to groom
themselves. Your pets will still need
your help to stay clean, however.
Regular grooming will keep
your guinea pigs healthy.

A winning smile

Gnawing on fruit-tree branches
will keep your pets' teeth
the right length. If their teeth
still grow too long, ask your
vet to shorten them.

A clean cage

Your pets will not be healthy
if their cage is dirty. Change
their wood shavings and hay
every day. Then wash their
bowl and water bottle. Once
a week, scrub the cage with
soapy water.

Fancy fur

To groom your guinea pigs, gently pull a brush along their coats in the direction that the fur grows. While you are brushing, check to make sure there are no insects living in the coat. You should also check that the eyes of your pets are clear and bright, and that their ears are clean. Your guinea pigs will also need occasional baths. To wash your pets, use only shampoo that has been given to you by your vet.

When choosing your guinea pigs, remember that long-haired guinea pigs require more work. They have to be groomed every day.

Play time!

Spend an hour every day playing with your pets. Play time will help your guinea pigs get used to you, and it will help them stay healthy. There are many toys you can buy that your pets will love. You can also make toys using materials you already have. These pages show some fun toys that your guinea pigs will enjoy.

One change at a time

Keep the cage interesting for your guinea pigs. Try adding new toys or moving toys from one area of the cage to another. Take your time making changes, though. If you switch too many things at once, your pets may become confused. A cardboard tube makes a great toy for your guinea pigs. They will enjoy crawling through it.

Guinea pigs enjoy playing
hide-and-seek. Cut a door in
a cardboard box to create a
fun place in which to hide.

Climbing on pieces of wood
is good exercise for your pets.
The wood is also fun to chew!

Use a large, clean rock to make
a hiding spot for your guinea
pigs. Your pets will crouch
behind it.

Colorful wooden toys are great for
pushing around and chewing.

Outside the cage

Guinea pigs are very curious. They enjoy spending time outside their cages. There are many things inside your house and in your yard that could hurt guinea pigs, however. Never leave your guinea pigs alone when they are loose in the house or in the yard.

In the house

Before taking your guinea pigs out of their cage, did you remember to:

- cover or remove all electrical wires?
- close all doors and windows?
- pick up any sharp objects?
- remove other pets from the room?
- let everyone in the house know that the guinea pigs are loose?

In the yard

When your pets are outdoors, do not forget that:

- other animals can seriously injure guinea pigs, so you should keep them in a fenced-in area.

- they should eat only grass and flowers that have not been sprayed with **pesticides.**

- direct sunlight and cold weather can make your guinea pigs sick, so let them play only in the shade and bring them inside after one hour.

Understanding your pets

Guinea pigs have their own ways of sending messages to you and to each other. They are very noisy animals! They may make chirping, squealing, or purring sounds. They also use **body language** to let others know what they are feeling.

A lot to say!

Guinea pigs make sounds for many reasons. They purr like kittens when they feel secure and happy. They may squeal loudly if they are scared or nervous. Your guinea pigs may also make chirping sounds if they are feeling friendly. By spending time with your pets, you will learn what each noise means.

The guinea pig on the right is nervous about meeting a new guinea pig. He is turning his head away and is standing very still.

Marking with scent

Guinea pigs have a good sense of smell. They rub their cheeks, backs, and bottoms on the things in their cage to leave their smells on them. Guinea pigs often sniff around to find their friends!

Ready to fight

If your guinea pigs are angry with one another, they will use body language to express it. Angry guinea pigs open their mouths wide to show their sharp teeth. Their fur might also stand on end, to make them look bigger and more threatening. If your guinea pigs get really angry, they might even fight.

Visiting a vet

A veterinarian is a medical doctor who treats animals. He or she will help you keep your guinea pigs healthy. You should take your new pets to the veterinarian as soon as you get them. Your vet can make sure the guinea pigs are healthy and answer any of your questions.

A yearly trip

Your pets should visit the vet every year for a checkup. The vet will check your guinea pigs and let you know if they are sick. He or she will also cut your guinea pigs' claws. Cutting claws must be done carefully. If the claws are cut too short, they will bleed.

When to get help

If you see any of the following changes in the body or behavior of one of your pets, take it to the vet.

 loses its fur

 sleeps more than usual

 has cloudy eyes or a runny nose

 drinks more water

 eats little or no food

vomits a lot

A long life

Remember to give your pets a clean home, good food, and a lot of love. If you keep your guinea pigs healthy, they will have happy, long lives with you.

Words to know

Note: Boldfaced words that are defined in the book may not appear on this page.

allergic Describing someone who has a physical reaction to something such as a food or animal dander

animal shelter A center that houses and cares for animals that do not have owners

body language Showing feelings by moving various body parts

breeder A person who brings guinea pigs together so they can make babies

ceramic Describing an object made of baked clay

gnaw To chew in order to wear down teeth

hutch A large wooden pen that houses small animals

pesticides Chemicals made to kill insects

veterinarian A medical doctor who treats animals

Index

1 2 3 4 5 6 7 8 9 0 Printed in the U.S.A. 3 2 1 0 9 8 7 6 5 4